PONCHOS
OPTIONS

LEISURE ARTS, INC.
Little Rock, Arkansas

EDITORIAL STAFF

Vice President and Editor-in-Chief: Sandra Graham Case. **Executive Director of Publications:** Cheryl Nodine Gunnells. **Senior Director of Publications:** Susan White Sullivan. **Director of Designer Relations:** Debra Nettles. **Director of Retail Marketing:** Stephen Wilson. **Art Operations Director:** Jeff Curtis. **Special Projects Coordinator:** Mary Sullivan Hutcheson. TECHNICAL — *Technical Writer:* Cathy Hardy. *Editorial Writer:* Susan McManus Johnson. ART — *Art Publications Director:* Rhonda Hodge Shelby. *Art Imaging Director:* Mark Hawkins. **Senior Publications Designer:** Dana Vaughn. *Imaging Technician:* Mark R. Potter. **Photography Stylist:** Cassie Francioni. **Contributing Photographer:** Jason Masters. *Publishing Systems Administrator:* Becky Riddle. **Publishing Systems Assistants:** Clint Hanson, Josh Hyatt, and John Rose.

BUSINESS STAFF

Chief Operating Officer: Tom Siebenmorgen. **Vice President, Sales and Marketing:** Pam Stebbins. **Director of Sales and Services:** Margaret Reinold. **Vice President, Operations:** Jim Dittrich. **Comptroller, Operations:** Rob Thieme. **Retail Customer Service Manager:** Stan Raynor. **Print Production Manager:** Fred F. Pruss.

Made in the United States of America.

ISBN 1-57486-586-2

PONCHOS
OPTIONS

Have you ever looked at a book of knit patterns and thought, "I like the design in this photo, but I wonder how would it look in another yarn?"

You don't have to wonder anymore. Leisure Arts' exciting new *Options* books actually let you see the results of alternative yarn choices. We create **each design twice**, using entirely different yarn brands and colors for the second version.

The delightful results in *Options: Ponchos* are a collection of 8 stylish garments in **two** variations by Margie Morse Pulley. Compare the options and prepare to be amazed at how many of these fashionable cover-ups you'll want to make. Whatever your skill level, our thorough instructions will have you finishing your ponchos with ease.

Your only question now should be,

"Which poncho will I knit first?"

Margie Morse Pulley

is a business owner, a wife, and a mother of three. She is also a witness to the connections between knitting, friendship, and miracles.

In 1999, Margie's daughter, then just six years old, became ill with an autoimmune disease that affected her eyes. Seemingly endless weeks of waiting began for Margie. She spent hours in doctor's offices and hospitals while her daughter received treatment. Through it all, knitting helped. "My mother sat with me and taught me the stitches," Margie says. "We called it 'medical knitting.' "

Just when life seemed to settle into a more normal routine, Margie was stunned to learn that she also suffers from an autoimmune disease. And once again, knitting was there for her.

"My blood work was done in the same facility where oncology patients are treated. To while away the time, I just kept thinking that when I felt better, I was going to do something I really loved. I decided I wanted to open a knitting shop. I told my husband what I had in mind. His support was immediate and has been unfailing ever since.

"So I prayed, 'Lord, is this what You want me to do?' And my answer came in the form of doors opening up to me. Only they didn't just open in the normal fashion — they *flew* open.

"The first thing I did was visit a friend who works at a local bank. I told him what I was thinking and I asked him if I could have a small business loan. To my surprise, he simply said 'okay.'

"The next step was finding a location. There was one in particular that I really wanted for my shop. I knew in my heart it was the right place, the perfect place for a yarn shop. And the day I went by to check on it was the very same day the owner placed a For Rent sign in the window.

"We opened Bella Lana Knitting in less than three months. That was eighteen months ago."

Smooth oak shelves line the walls of the new shop. Each compartment offers an abundance of fine yarn. The tempting skeins have become a familiar indulgence for many of Margie's regular customers. The wealth of color and texture also bring in passersby who are delighted to learn that they, too, can knit.

In the center of the store are a large table and a generous number of chairs. This is where Margie's customers gather for classes and the once-a-month Ladies' Night Out. And the table is often occupied by customers who just drop by to visit.

"The most unusual friendships get started when knitting is involved," says Margie. "My nineteen-year-old shop assistant has become a bosom buddy to a regular customer who is in her early sixties. And right now," Margie indicates three ladies currently at the table, "the wife of a missionary to Nigeria, a former Madison Avenue executive, and my assistant are all knitting and whooping it up over there." As if on cue, there is a burst of laughter and loud conversation.

The shop does seem to be an answered prayer for Margie, who continues to knit for relaxation as well as for physical therapy. There is a metal plate in her hand, a result of her illness. "Knitting is the perfect exercise for my hand," she says. "It keeps it from hurting."

Margie also found herself knitting out of necessity. "When we opened the shop, it seemed there were very few knitting patterns for beginners. So I started designing easy scarves and worked my way up. Now that ponchos are popular again, I've designed several in simple patterns.

> "...while knitting enables you to create a great garment, it can also help you build some amazing friendships."

"I think people enjoy the results of knitting because it's fun to see someone's jaw drop when they realize you made the poncho, scarf, or sweater you're wearing. And it's even better to see someone you love wearing something you made for them.

"Knitting really is the new yoga, the new left brain/right brain exercise. And while knitting enables you to create a great garment, it can also help you build some amazing friendships."

Judging by the enthusiastic outbursts at the shop's worktable, Margie's customers couldn't agree more.

CONTENTS

A LITTLE LUXURY

OPTION

1

If you adore the **richness** of **fur** and love a project that knits up quickly, then this pink poncho will be your new fashion favorite. It goes **everywhere**, and with anything you want to wear.

Then again, there's much to be said for the opulence of **precious metals**. The same pattern in a **metallic** yarn also finishes in a flash. And this elegant wrap will reflect the gleam of **admiring eyes** wherever you go.

OPTION 2

Moda Dea™ Fur Ever™
Bulky Weight Novelty Eyelash Yarn
   [1³/₄ ounces, 49 yards (50 grams, 45 meters)
   per skein]:
   #3743 Pinksuasion - 5 skeins

Straight knitting needles, size 15 (10 mm)
Yarn needle

A LITTLE LUXURY ◖█▢▢ EASY

Trendsetter Yarns® Sorbet
Medium Weight Novelty Yarn
   [1³/₄ ounces, 55 yards (50 grams, 50.5 meters)
   per skein]:
   #1028 Neutrals - 4 skeins

Straight knitting needles, size 15 (10 mm)
Yarn needle

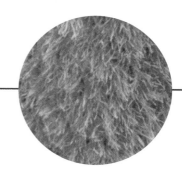

Poncho

Cast on 36 sts.

Row 1: K1, (YO, K2 tog) across to last st *(Figs. 4 & 5, page 44)*, K1.

Repeat Row 1 for pattern until piece measures approximately 60" (152.5 cm) from cast on edge.

Bind off all sts in knit.

Finishing

Fold piece in half widthwise. Beginning at cast on/bind off edge, weave one long edge together for 18" (45.5 cm) **or** until desired opening for neck *(Fig. 7, page 45)*.

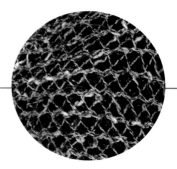

CATCH OF THE DAY

OPTION

1

Cast your net and catch a fashion treasure! This **ultra-soft** poncho in rust is knitted in an open, **easy fishnet** pattern and has a crocheted edging. You'll be glad this accessory is one that didn't get away!

The same "fishnet" poncho is imminently **eyecatching** in white! It's a perfect wardrobe accent for **cool summer evenings**. And in warmer regions, it will **bridge the seasons** with style.

② OPTION

Option 1

Lion Brand® Chenille "Thick & Quick"® Super Bulky Weight Yarn
   [100 yards (91.4 meters) per skein]:
   #135 Terracotta - 4 skeins

Straight knitting needles, size 19 (15 mm)
Crochet hook, size Q (15 mm) for Edging
Yarn needle

CATCH OF THE DAY ■■■□ INTERMEDIATE

Option 2

Coats & Clark® Grandé
Super Bulky Weight Yarn
   [6 ounces, 149 yards (170 grams, 136 meters)
   per skein]:
   #2101 White - 3 skeins

Straight knitting needles, size 19 (15 mm)
Crochet hook, size Q (15 mm) for Edging
Yarn needle

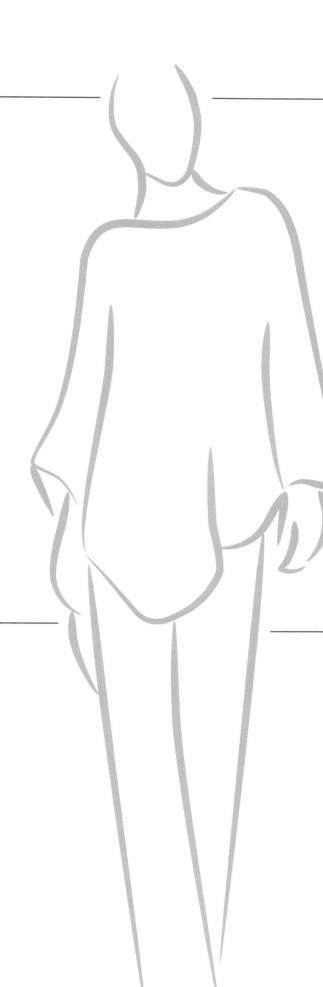

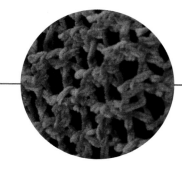

Poncho

Cast on 34 sts.

Row 1 (Right side)**:** Knit across.

Row 2: Purl across.

Row 3: K2, (YO, K2 tog) across to last 2 sts *(Figs. 4 & 5, page 44)*, K2.

Row 4: P2, P1 tbl *(Fig. 3, page 44)*, (P1, P1 tbl) across to last 3 sts, P3.

Row 5: K2, (K2 tog, YO) across to last 2 sts, K2.

Row 6: P3, P1 tbl, (P1, P1 tbl) across to last 2 sts, P2.

Repeat Rows 3-6 for pattern until piece measures approximately 66" (167.5 cm) from cast on edge, ending by working Row 4 or Row 6.

Last Row: Knit across.

Bind off all sts in purl.

Finishing

With **wrong** side together, fold piece in half widthwise. Beginning at cast on/bind off edge, weave one long edge together for 18" (45.5 cm) **or** until desired opening for neck *(Fig. 7, page 45)*.

EDGING

With **right** side facing and working around bottom edge with a crochet hook, join yarn with sc at seam *(see Crochet Stitches, pages 46 & 47)*; sc evenly around; join with slip st to first sc, finish off.

BELLA STRIPE

OPTION

1

Add this comfortable wrap to your list of **weekend wear**! You can rely upon the denim-colored shadings and tasseled corners to pair well with all your favorite **blue jeans**. And the warmth of wool will be welcome, whether you **relax** with friends or hurry to complete **Saturday** errands.

Choose two **spirited hues**, then simply turn your completed Bella Stripe poncho to one side — now you have an entirely **different look** from the same pattern! Wear the colors of your alma mater, or adorn yourself in the shades that bring out **your beauty**. The choice is entirely yours.

OPTION 2

Option 1

Lion Brand® Wool-Ease® Thick & Quick® **SUPER BULKY 6**
Super Bulky Weight Yarn
  [6 ounces, 108 yards (170 grams, 98 meters)
  per skein]:
  Color A: #114 Denim - 2 skeins
  Color B: #194 Denim Twist - 2 skeins

Straight knitting needles, size 19 (15 mm) **or**
  size needed for gauge
Crochet hook, size Q (15 mm) for Edging
Yarn needle

GAUGE: In Stockinette Stitch,
     6 sts and 8 rows = 4" (10 cm)

BELLA STRIPE  BEGINNER

Option 2

Rowan Int.® Big Wool **SUPER BULKY 6**
Super Bulky Weight Yarn
  [3¹/₂ ounces, 87 yards (100 grams, 80 meters)
  per skein]:
  Color A: #029 Pistachio - 2 skeins
  Color B: #014 Whoosh - 2 skeins

Straight knitting needles, size 19 (15 mm) **or**
  size needed for gauge
Crochet hook, size Q (15 mm) for Edging
Yarn needle

GAUGE: In Stockinette Stitch,
     6 sts and 8 rows = 4" (10 cm)

Poncho

With Color A, cast on 32 sts.

Work in Stockinette Stitch (knit one row, purl one row) in the following color sequence: 18 rows of Color A, (18 rows of Color B, 18 rows of Color A) 3 times.

Bind off all sts.

Finishing

With **wrong** side together, fold piece in half widthwise. Beginning at cast on/bind off edge, weave one long edge together across two stripes **or** until desired opening for neck (*Fig. 7, page 45*).

EDGING

With **right** side facing and working across un-joined long edge with a crochet hook, join Color A with slip st at corner (*see Crochet Stitches, pages 46 & 47*); slip st evenly across; finish off.

TASSELS

Cut a piece of cardboard 2" (5 cm) square. Wind a double strand of Color B around the cardboard approximately 10 times. Cut an 18" (45.5 cm) length of yarn and insert it under all of the strands at the top of the cardboard; pull up **tightly** and tie securely. Leave the yarn ends long enough to attach the tassel. Cut the yarn at the opposite end of the cardboard and then remove it (*Fig. 1a*). Cut a 12" (30.5 cm) length of yarn and wrap it **tightly** around the tassel twice, 1" (2.5 cm) below the top (*Fig. 1b*); tie securely. Trim the ends.

Make a total of 9 tassels. Using photo as a guide for placement, attach tassels around outer edge, placing one at seam, each corner, and between stripes.

Fig. 1a

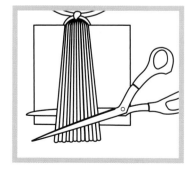

Fig. 1b

BARELY THERE OPTION 1

Sometimes, all you need is a whisper of **romance** … or perhaps a hint of **mystery**. This openwork shawl embodies both in its elegant drape and wispy, trailing fringe.

Now you see it. Now you don't. The **mingled** colors of a variegated yarn draw the eye, while the airy design calls attention to what you're wearing beneath this sweetly hued, **barely there** wrap. It's a fashion classic that **reveals** everything wonderful about you.

Option 1

Classic Elite Yarns® Provence
Medium Weight Cotton Yarn
  [$3^{1}/_{2}$ ounces, 205 yards (100 grams, 186 meters)
  per skein]:
    #5201 White - 3 skeins

Straight knitting needles, size 11 (8 mm)
Yarn needle

MEDIUM 4

BARELY THERE   ◖■■■▭ INTERMEDIATE

Option 2

TLC® Cotton Plus™
Medium Weight Cotton Blend Yarn
  [3 ounces, 155 yards (85 grams, 140 meters)
  per skein]:
  #3615 Jazz - 3 skeins

Straight knitting needles, size 11 (8 mm)
Yarn needle

MEDIUM 4

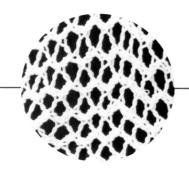

Poncho

Cast on 56 sts.

Row 1 (Right side)**:** Knit across.

Row 2: Purl across.

Row 3: K7, (K2 tog, YO) across to last st (*Figs. 4 & 5, page 44*), K1.

Row 4: (P1, P1 tbl) across to last 8 sts (*Fig. 3, page 44*), P8.

Row 5: K7, (YO, K2 tog) across to last st, K1.

Row 6: P2, P1 tbl, (P1, P1 tbl) across to last 7 sts, P7.

Repeat Rows 3-6 for pattern until piece measures approximately 52" (132 cm) from cast on edge, ending by working Row 4 or Row 6.

Next Row: Knit across.

Last Row: Purl across.

K6, bind off remaining sts in knit: 6 sts.

Finishing
FRINGE

Slowly unravel the 6 edge sts on every row, one row at a time, tying an overhand knot close to poncho using 2 loops; cut loops.

With **wrong** side together, fold piece in half widthwise. Beginning at cast on/bind off edge, weave long unfringed edge together for 13" (33 cm) **or** until desired opening for neck (*Fig. 7, page 45*).

OPTION 1

RIBBONS OF COLOR

Keep your options open with this colorful ribbon yarn creation. Wear it with the longest points **in front**, in the style of an old-fashioned pelerine. Or turn your **ribbon poncho** to make the stripes run vertically over your shoulders, creating a shortened mantle.

What a difference a change of yarn makes! The **dramatic** pink and black stripes of this wrap drape gracefully from the shoulders. Augmented only with **short tassels** for an extra bit of flair, this is a **go-everywhere** fashion that will get you noticed!

OPTION 2

Lion Brand® Incredible
Super Bulky Weight Ribbon Yarn **SUPER BULKY 6**
[1³/₄ ounces, 110 yards (50 grams, 100 meters) per ball]:
Color A: #202 Blue Shades - 5 balls
Color B: #205 Carnival - 2 balls

Straight knitting needles, size 10 (6 mm) **or**
size needed for gauge
Yarn needle

GAUGE: In Stockinette Stitch,
13 sts = 4" (10 cm)

RIBBONS OF COLOR ◖◼◻◻ EASY

Option 2

Trendsetter Yarns® Dolcino **MEDIUM 4**
Medium Weight Ribbon Yarn
[1³/₄ ounces, 99 yards (50 grams, 90 meters) per ball]:
Color A: #101 Black - 4 balls
Color B: #25 Pink - 3 balls

Straight knitting needles, size 10 (6 mm) **or**
size needed for gauge
Yarn needle

GAUGE: In Stockinette Stitch,
13 sts = 4" (10 cm)

Poncho

With Color A, cast on 45 sts.

Row 1 (Right side)**:** K9, (M1, K9) across (*Figs. 6a & b, page 45*): 49 sts.

Row 2: Purl across.

Work in Stockinette Stitch (knit one row, purl one row) in the following color sequence: 14 Rows of Color A, (10 rows of Color B, 16 rows of Color A) 9 times.

Note: After dropping a stitch to be used for a lattice pattern, the next stitch should be bound off **very** *loosely.*

Bind off first 8 sts, (drop next st, bind off next 9 sts) across: 4 dropped sts.

Slowly unravel the dropped stitches down the entire length of piece forming a lattice.

Finishing

With **wrong** side together, fold piece in half widthwise. Beginning at cast on/bind off edge, weave one long edge together for 16" (40.5 cm) **or** until desired opening for neck (*Fig. 7, page 45*).

TASSELS

Cut a piece of cardboard 2" (5 cm) square.

You will need 68 yards of Color A. If you run short on ribbon yarn, adjust the size of each Tassel.

Measure and cut 6 yards (5.5 meters) of Color A. Fold the length in half and wind the doubled ribbon yarn around the cardboard. Cut a 16" (40.5 cm) length of ribbon yarn and insert it under all of the strands at the top of the cardboard; pull up **tightly** and tie securely. Leave the ends long enough to attach the tassel. Slide the cardboard out. Cut a 12" (30.5 cm) length of ribbon yarn and wrap it **tightly** around the tassel twice, 1" (2.5 cm) below the top; tie securely. Cut the ribbon loops at the bottom of the tassel (*Fig. 1b, page 19*). Trim the ends.

Make a total of 10 tassels.

Using photo as a guide for placement, attach tassels around outer edge, placing one at center of each Color A stripe.

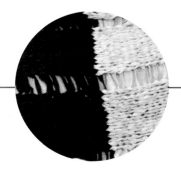

FOREVER FASHIONABLE

OPTION

1

Put a little **zing** in your winter with hues from the spice rack! The back-to nature colors of a variegated yarn remind the viewer of **curry** and **chili**, a blend that really heats up when **fur-textured** yarn is added to the fringe edging and the simple tie closure. Warm, soft, and comforting — this is a poncho you'll want to wear **all season**.

Except for a change of yarn, this cozy olive and gray poncho is the same **toasty creation** as Option One. However, there's a fun **secret** to creating the fluffy fringe on **both** these Forever fashions. It's a simple technique that lets you finish your poncho in a **jiffy**!

OPTION 2

Option 1

Lion Brand® Jiffy® Thick & Quick®
Super Bulky Weight Yarn
[5 ounces, 84 yards (140 grams, 76 meters)
per skein]:
#212 Adirondacks - 4 skeins
Lion Brand® Fun Fur
Bulky Weight Eyelash Yarn
[$1^3/_4$ ounces, 64 yards (50 grams, 58 meters)
per skein]:
#134 Copper - 2 skeins

Straight knitting needles, size 17 (12.75 mm)
Crochet hook, size K (6.5 cm) for tie and fringe
Yarn needle

FOREVER FASHIONABLE EASY

Option 2

Jaeger® Natural Fleece
Super Bulky Weight Yarn
[$3^1/_2$ ounces, 93 yards (100 grams, 85 meters)
per skein]:
#529 Olivine - 3 skeins
Jaeger® Fur
Super Bulky Weight Fur Yarn
[$1^3/_4$ ounces, 22 yards (50 grams, 20 meters)
per skein]: #053 Jaguar - 4 skeins

Straight knitting needles, size 17 (12.75 mm)
Crochet hook, size K (6.5 cm) for tie and fringe
Yarn needle

Poncho

Holding one strand of each yarn together, cast on 36 sts.

Rows 1-4: Knit across.

Row 5 (Right side)**:** K6, drop eyelash/fur to front, K1, (YO, K2 tog) across to last st (*Figs. 4 & 5, page 44*), K1.

Row 6: K1, (YO, K2 tog) across to last 7 sts, K1, pick up eyelash/fur, K6 using both yarns.

Repeat Rows 5 and 6 for pattern until piece measures approximately 50" (127 cm) from cast on edge, ending by working Row 6.

Using both yarns, K5, cut and secure eyelash/fur, bind off remaining sts in knit: 5 sts.

Finishing
FRINGE

Slowly unravel the 5 edge sts on every row, one row at a time, tying an overhand knot close to poncho using one loop of each yarn; cut loops.

ADDITIONAL FRINGE

Cut a piece of cardboard 8" (20.5 cm) square. Wind the yarn **loosely** and **evenly** around the cardboard until the card is filled, then cut across one end; repeat as needed with both yarns. Hold one strand of each yarn together; fold in half. With **wrong** side facing and using a crochet hook, draw the folded end up through a stitch on cast on edge and pull the loose ends through the folded end (*Fig. 2a*); draw the knot up **tightly** (*Fig. 2b*). Repeat for each stitch.
Lay flat on a hard surface and trim the ends.

Using diagram as a guide, sew the bound off edge to the lower left side, matching the fringed edges.

TIE

Holding one strand of each yarn together and using a crochet hook, make a chain 60" (152.5 cm) long (*Fig. 9, page 46*).

Positioning the point to be at the front, weave chain through stitches around the neck edge to form a gathered neck closure.

Fig. 2a

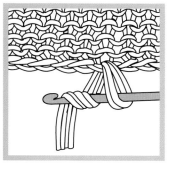

Fig. 2b

DIAGRAM

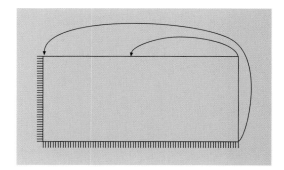

OPTION

RICHNESS ALL AROUND

1

When warmth and fashion blend together so well, your **comfort** is only eclipsed by your **confidence**! This rich **wool** and fur-textured yarn creation displays the **fur yarn** along its edges in a design meant to pamper your senses. **Lucky you!**

The stretchy quality of **chenille** yarn gives the same pattern a **lacy** look, but still retains a **plush** feel. Lime-colored fur yarn stands out against the blue. It's a **tropical treat** in a cool-weather wrap — a contrast you'll appreciate as the season progresses.

OPTION 2

Rowan Int.® Big Wool
Super Bulky Weight Yarn
[3¹/₂ ounces, 87 yards (100 grams, 80 meters) per skein]:
#008 Black - 5 skeins

SUPER BULKY 6

Jaeger® Fur
Super Bulky Weight Fur Yarn
[1³/₄ ounces, 22 yards (50 grams, 20 meters) per skein]:
#053 Jaguar - 2 skeins

SUPER BULKY 6

Straight knitting needles, size 19 (15 mm) **or** size needed for gauge
Yarn needle

GAUGE: In Stockinette Stitch,
6 sts and 8 rows = 4" (10 cm)

RICHNESS ALL AROUND ◖◼◻◻◻◗ BEGINNER

Lion Brand® Chenille "Thick & Quick® Prints"
Super Bulky Weight Fur Yarn
[75 yards (68.5 meters) per skein]:
#209 Tropical Fish - 4 skeins

SUPER BULKY 6

Lion Brand® Fun Fur
Bulky Weight Eyelash Yarn
[1.75 ounces, 64 yards (50 grams, 58 meters) per skein]:
#194 Lime - 1 skein

BULKY 5

Straight knitting needles, size 19 (15 mm) **or** size needed for gauge
Yarn needle

GAUGE: In Stockinette Stitch,
6 sts and 8 rows = 4" (10 cm)

Poncho

Holding one strand of each yarn together, cast on 32 sts.

Row 1 (Right side)**:** Knit across.

Row 2: Purl across.

Rows 3 and 4: Repeat Rows 1 and 2.

Row 5: K3, drop eyelash/fur to **front**, knit across.

Row 6: Purl across to last 3 sts, pick up fur, K3 using both yarns.

Repeat Rows 5 and 6 for pattern until piece measures approximately 58" (147.5 cm) from cast on edge, ending by working Row 6.

Using both yarns, repeat Rows 1 and 2 twice.

Bind off all sts in knit.

Finishing

With **wrong** side together, fold piece in half widthwise. Beginning at cast on/bind off edge, weave long edge without eyelash/fur together for 16" (40.5 cm) **or** until desired opening for neck (*Fig. 7, page 45*).

AN EYE FOR BEAUTY

OPTION

1

One of the best things about knitting is that a **simple** garment, fashioned using ordinary **stockinette** stitch, can absolutely **glow with beauty**. All it takes is an interesting yarn like this super bulky eyelash to make your one-of-a-kind poncho **as fun as you want it** to be!

Here's your daily serving of citrus! This **tangy little poncho** is quickly created using a variegated, bulky weight eyelash yarn. You can **dress it up or down** to fit the occasion. As with most of the ponchos in this collection, you get a **variety** of looks by wearing the tapered end behind you, in front of you, or at one side.

2

OPTION

Crystal Palace Yarns® Splash
Super Bulky Weight Short Eyelash Yarn
  [$3^1/_2$ ounces, 85 yards (100 grams,
  77.5 meters) per skein]:
  #3388 Garnet - 3 skeins

Straight knitting needles, size 15 (10 mm)
Yarn needle

AN EYE FOR BEAUTY ■■□□ EASY

Bernat® Boa
Bulky Weight Short Eyelash Yarn
  [$1^3/_4$ ounces, 71 yards (50 grams, 65 meters)
  per skein]:
  #81605 Tweety Bird - 4 skeins

Straight knitting needles, size 15 (10 mm)
Yarn needle

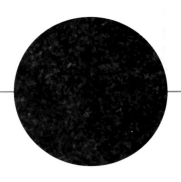

Poncho

Cast on 36 sts.

Work in Stockinette Stitch (knit one row, purl one row) until piece measures approximately 50" (127 cm) from cast on edge.

Bind off all sts.

Finishing

Using diagram as a guide, sew the bound off edge to the lower left side.

DIAGRAM

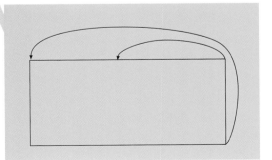

What is GAUGE?

Gauge simply means "the number of stitches per inch."

To understand why stitch size is important, imagine for a moment that three knitters decided to make the same poncho. They each decide to use the same yarn and same size needles as their neighbors. Would their ponchos be identical in size when finished? Probably not. Each of the three knitters will naturally use a different tension on the yarn while knitting, so her stitches may be larger or smaller than her neighbors'.

When is gauge important?

For the designs in this collection, you only need to check your gauge when you create a poncho using Stockinette Stitch. This stitch tends to be very stable, giving you almost no "stretch" in your finished garment. For these ponchos, a gauge is given at the bottom of the supply lists.

But getting the gauge right is REALLY EASY. Go ahead and make a sample swatch for your Stockinette Stitch poncho using the yarn and needle specified. When your swatch is the size listed, count the stitches and rows (if rows are called for). If your swatch is larger or smaller than the gauge given, change needle size and make another swatch. Repeat this until you have determined the correct needle size to get the specified gauge. It's just that simple!

KNITTING GAUGE
6" RULER
2" STITCH MEASURE

INSTRUCTIONS: To check your needle size recommended in Smooth out swatch and pin stitch measure over swatch a number of rows down. If you for in the instructions, use smaller needles. Knit new sw

0 1 2 3 4 5 6 7 8 9 10

Why don't I need to make a sample swatch before I knit any of the other ponchos?

For most of the ponchos in this collection, no gauge size is given. This is because these designs tend to have a little bit of stretch in the finished fabric. Your poncho may be a little larger or smaller than the one in the photograph without changing its overall appearance. Just use the yarn weight and the needle size specified. Consider purchasing an extra skein of yarn in the event you decide your poncho needs to be longer, but remember to ask about the store's return policy regarding unused skeins.

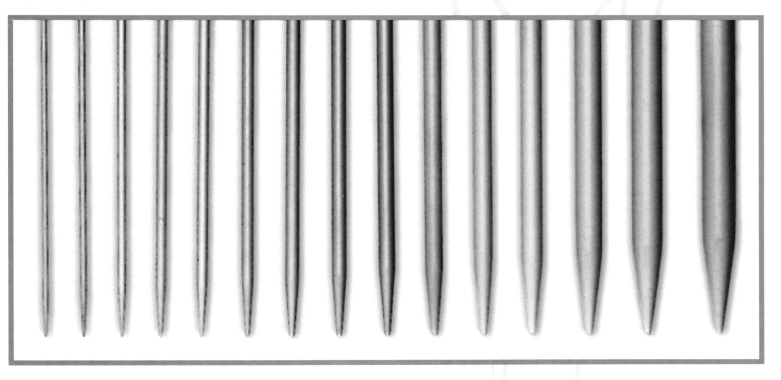

GENERAL

ABBREVIATIONS

cm	centimeters
K	knit
M1	make one
mm	millimeters
P	purl
sc	single crochet(s)
st(s)	stitch(es)
tbl	through back loop
tog	together
YO	yarn over

( ) or [ ] — work enclosed instructions **as many times** as specified by the number immediately following **or** contains explanatory remarks.

colon (:) — the number(s) given after a colon at the end of a row or round denote(s) the number of stitches or spaces you should have on that row or round.

KNITTING NEEDLES

Aluminum: Aluminum needles do not bend or break, and they make a clicking sound as you knit. Their smooth surface rarely develops fiber-catching burrs, and many aluminum needles are treated with protective finishes to insure durability.

Plastic: Plastic needles are lightweight, less slippery than aluminum and make less noise when knitting. When knitting with a slippery yarn such as a brushed acrylic, rayon, or a ribbon yarn, you may find the stitches easier to control on plastic needles.

Bamboo: Bamboo needles have a polished, smooth surface, are lightweight, and tap quietly as you knit. Extra care is required to prevent scratches on the shaft of these needles that could snag your yarn.

INSTRUCTIONS

KNITTING NEEDLES		
UNITED STATES	**ENGLISH U.K.**	**METRIC (mm)**
0	13	2
1	12	2.25
2	11	2.75
3	10	3.25
4	9	3.5
5	8	3.75
6	7	4
7	6	4.5
8	5	5
9	4	5.5
10	3	6
10½	2	6.5
11	1	8
13	00	9
15	000	10
17	---	12.75
19	---	15

KNIT & CROCHET TERMINOLOGY		
UNITED STATES		**INTERNATIONAL**
gauge	=	tension
bind off	=	cast off
yarn over (YO)	=	yarn forward (yfwd) **or** yarn around needle (yrn)
slip stitch (slip st)	=	single crochet (sc)
single crochet (sc)	=	double crochet (dc)

Yarn Weight Symbol & Names	SUPER FINE 1	FINE 2	LIGHT 3	MEDIUM 4	BULKY 5	SUPER BULKY 6
Type of Yarns in Category	Sock, Fingering Baby	Sport, Baby	DK, Light Worsted	Worsted, Afghan, Aran	Chunky, Craft, Rug	Bulky, Roving
Knit Gauge Ranges in Stockinette St to 4" (10 cm)	27-32 sts	23-26 sts	21-24 sts	16-20 sts	12-15 sts	6-11 sts
Advised Needle Size Range	1-3	3-5	5-7	7-9	9-11	11 and larger

■□□□ **BEGINNER**		Projects for first-time knitters using basic knit and purl stitches. Minimal shaping.
■■□□ **EASY**		Projects using basic stitches, repetitive stitch patterns, simple color changes, and simple shaping and finishing.
■■■□ **INTERMEDIATE**		Projects with a variety of stitches, such as basic cables and lace, simple intarsia, double-pointed needles and knitting in the round needle techniques, mid-level shaping and finishing.
■■■■ **EXPERIENCED**		Projects using advanced techniques and stitches. such as short rows, fair isle, more intricate intarsia, cables, lace patterns, and numerous color changes.

PURL ONE THROUGH BACK LOOP

(abbreviated P1 tbl)

Insert the **right** needle through the back loop of the next stitch *(Fig. 3)* and purl it.

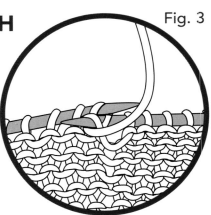

Fig. 3

YARN OVER

(abbreviated YO)

Bring the yarn forward **between** the needles, then back **over** the top of the right hand needle, so that it is now in position to knit the next stitch *(Fig. 4)*.

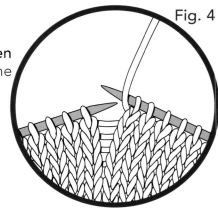

Fig. 4

KNIT 2 TOGETHER

(abbreviated K2 tog)

Insert the right needle into the **front** of the first two stitches on the left needle as if to **knit** *(Fig. 5)*, then **knit** them together as if they were one stitch.

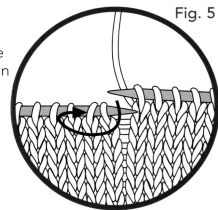

Fig. 5

MAKE ONE
(abbreviated M1)
Insert the **left** needle under the horizontal strand between the stitches from the front *(Fig. 6a)*. Then knit into the **back** of the strand *(Fig. 6b)*.

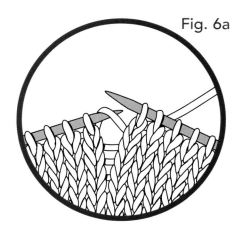
Fig. 6a

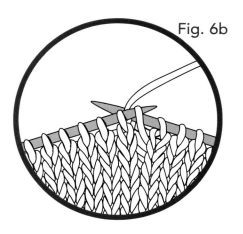
Fig. 6b

WEAVING SEAMS
With the **right** side of both pieces facing you and edges even, sew through both sides once to secure the seam. Insert the needle under the bar **between** the first and second stitches on the row and pull the yarn through *(Fig. 7)*. Insert the needle under the next bar on the second side. Repeat from side to side, being careful to match rows.

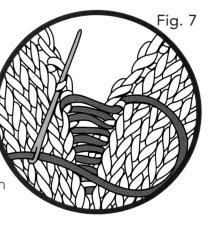
Fig. 7

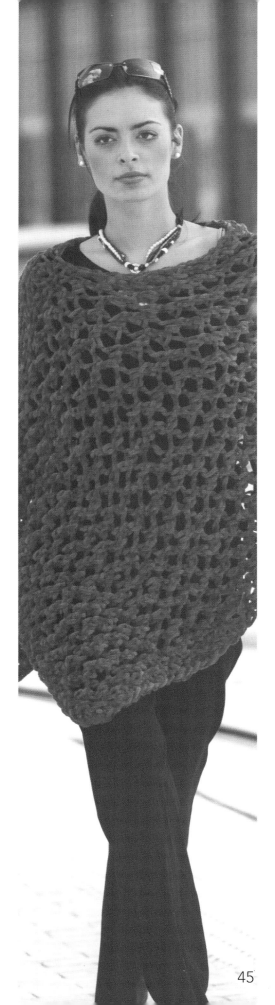

BASIC CROCHET STTICHES
YARN OVER
(abbreviated YO)
Bring the yarn over the top of the hook from back to front, catching the yarn with the hook and turning the hook slightly toward you to keep the yarn from slipping off *(Fig. 8)*.

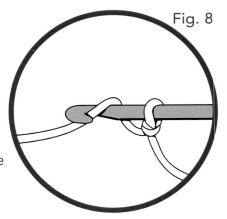

Fig. 8

CHAIN
YO, draw the yarn through the stitch on hook *(Fig. 9)*.

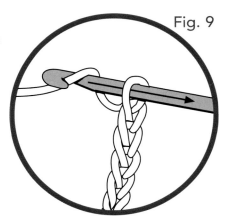

Fig. 9

SINGLE CROCHET
(abbreviated sc)
Insert hook in stitch indicated, YO and pull up a loop, YO and draw through both loops on hook *(Fig. 10)*.

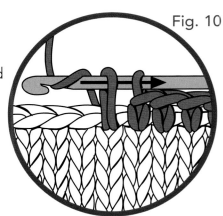

Fig. 10

JOINING WITH SC

Begin with a slip knot on the hook. Insert hook in stitch indicated, YO and pull up a loop, YO and draw through both loops on hook (*Fig. 11*).

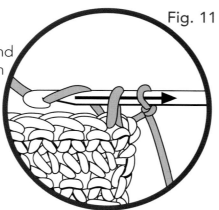

Fig. 11

SLIP STITCH

   (*abbreviated slip st*)
Insert hook in stitch indicated, YO and draw through loop on hook (*Fig. 12*).

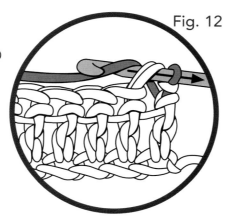

Fig. 12

HINTS AND TIPS
GARTER STITCH
Garter Stitch is the result of knitting every stitch in every row. Two rows of knitting make one horizontal ridge in your fabric (Photo A).

Photo A

STOCKINETTE STITCH
Stockinette Stitch is the result of alternating knit and purl rows. The right side is smooth (Photo B) and the wrong side is bumpy (Photo C).

Photo B

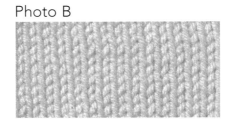

Photo C

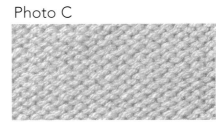

YARN ENDS
As in all garments, good finishing techniques make a big difference in the quality of the piece. Do not tie knots. Always start a new ball at the beginning of a row, leaving ends long enough to weave in later.
Thread a yarn needle with the yarn end. With wrong side facing, weave the needle through several inches, then reverse the direction and weave it back through several inches. When ends are secure, clip them off close to work.

BINDING OFF
Count stitches as you bind off: It takes two stitches to bind off one stitch. Count each stitch as you bind it off, not as you knit it.
Binding off in pattern: Unless otherwise stated, when you are instructed to bind off your stitches, you should always bind off in pattern. In reality, you are working another row.
Binding off loosely versus tightly: Bind off loosely for an edge with elasticity and bind off tightly for a firm edge.